# BAA

by Roger Hargreaves

HODDER AND STOUGHTON
LONDON SYDNEY AUCKLAND TORONTO

Baa was a sort of sheep.
A Timbuctoo sheep.
And a very old sheep indeed.
She had lived in Lambstail Cottage.
In Timbuctoo.
For years and years and years.

She was so old she was a little short-sighted.
And couldn't see as well as she used to.
And she was a little hard of hearing.
She couldn't hear as well as she used to.

TIMBUCTOO

One day she was out walking when she met Woof.
Woof was a sort of dog.
"Hello," said Woof.
"Hello," said Baa, peering over her glasses. "Who are you?"

"I'm a dog," said Woof.
"You don't look a bit like a frog," said Baa.
And went on her way.

She met Meow.
Meow was a sort of cat.
"Hello," said Meow.
"Hello," said Baa, peering over her glasses. "Who are you?"

"I'm a cat," said Meow.
"Yes you are getting fat," said Baa.
And went on her way.

She met Squeak.
Squeak was a sort of mouse.
"Hello," said Squeak.
"Hello," said Baa, peering over her glasses. "Who are you?"

"I'm a mouse," said Squeak.
"You can't be a house," said Baa.
"You haven't got a chimney!"

The reason Baa was out for a walk was because she was going shopping.
She wanted to buy herself a ball of wool so that she could knit a new woolly jacket.
And she wanted to buy some bread for her tea.

She went into the shop.
"I'd like a ball of wool," she said.
"But this is the bread shop," said the shopkeeper.
"We only sell bread!"
"No. No," said Baa, "I don't want thread, I want wool. A ball of wool!"

"But," replied the shopkeeper, "the only thing we have is bread!"

"Don't be silly," said Baa. "Of course I don't want to go to bed!"

"But . . ." said the shopkeeper.

"You're shut?" said Baa. "Then you can't sell me a ball of wool can you!" And she left, and went into the shop next door.
The wool shop.

"A large white loaf please," said Baa.
"But we only sell wool," replied the shopkeeper.
"Pull?" said Baa. "Pull what?"
"No, no," said the shopkeeper, "I didn't say that!"
"A hat?" said Baa. "I don't want a hat. I want some bread."

"But . ." said the shopkeeper.
"Oh you're shut as well are you?"
said Baa.
And went home.

On her way Baa met Cluck.
Cluck was a sort of hen.
"Who are you?" asked Baa, peering over the top of her glasses.
"I'm a hen," said Cluck.

"You're ten?" said Baa.
"I'm much older than you!"